A Crabtree Branches Book

Today's Stars

BEYONCÉ

Ellen Rodger

Crabtree Publishing
crabtreebooks.com

School-to-Home Support for Caregivers and Teachers

This high-interest book is designed to motivate striving students with engaging topics while building fluency, vocabulary, and an interest in reading. Here are a few questions and activities to help the reader build upon his or her comprehension skills.

Before Reading:

- *What do I think this book is about?*
- *What do I know about this topic?*
- *What do I want to learn about this topic?*
- *Why am I reading this book?*

During Reading:

- *I wonder why...*
- *I'm curious to know...*
- *How is this like something I already know?*
- *What have I learned so far?*

After Reading:

- *What was the author trying to teach me?*
- *What are some details?*
- *How did the photographs and captions help me understand more?*
- *Read the book again and look for the vocabulary words.*
- *What questions do I still have?*

Extension Activities:

- *What was your favorite part of the book? Write a paragraph on it.*
- *Draw a picture of your favorite thing you learned from the book.*

TABLE OF CONTENTS

QUEEN BEY

Not every artist is recognized by just their first name. But Beyoncé is. She is a singer, songwriter, dancer, actress, businessperson, and producer. Beyoncé was **destined** for superstardom.

Beyoncé is often called Queen Bey. Her mega-fans are called the BeyHive.

Beyoncé is considered one of the most **influential** people of this century. What she says and does are important. Beyoncé shapes people's opinions about music and the world.

Reinventing herself is one of Beyoncé's many skills. She performs in multiple music **genres**. She manages many aspects of her business. Beyoncé has also won hundreds of awards for her work.

Fun Facts

In 2016, Beyoncé's album *Lemonade* won a Peabody Award. Peabodys recognize excellence in storytelling. *Lemonade* was called "a stunningly beautiful masterpiece."

CHILD OF DESTINY

Beyoncé Giselle Knowles was born on September 4, 1981, in Houston, Texas. She is the first child of Tina and Mathew Knowles. Her parents raised her and younger sister Solange in Houston.

Solange is also a successful singer-songwriter, dancer, actress, and businessperson.

As a young child, Beyoncé showed an interest and talent for music and dance. She took dance lessons and sang at church. At seven, Beyoncé won her school talent show. She also joined her school choir.

Beyoncé was shy as a child, but dance and singing competitions helped her grow up to be a confident performer.

When Beyoncé was nine, she auditioned and won a place in an all-girl group. The group was called Girl's Tyme. Members sang, rapped, and danced at events around the Houston area.

Girl's Tyme was formed in 1990.

Fun Facts

Girl's Tyme appeared on *Star Search*, the largest talent show on American television. They didn't win. However, the experience helped shape Beyoncé's desire to be the best she could be.

GROUP WORK

Beyoncé's parents believed in her talent. Her father quit his job to manage Girl's Tyme. Soon the group had a recording contract and changed its name to Destiny's Child.

Beyoncé's Destiny's Child bandmates were Michelle Williams and Kelly Rowland.

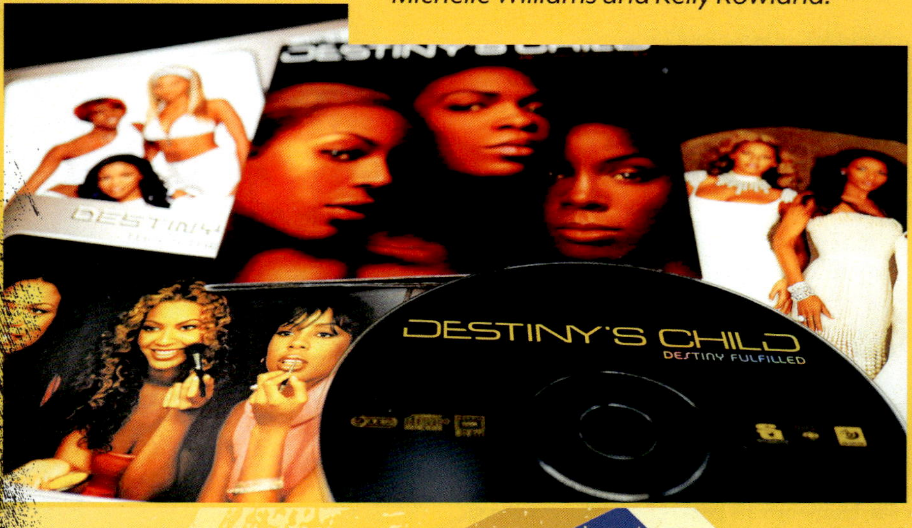

Destiny's Child released five albums from 1998 to 2004. The group won dozens of awards, including three **Grammy Awards**.

While performing with Destiny's Child, Beyoncé also launched an acting career. She started out in musicals and comedies and quickly moved on to musical dramas.

Beyoncé starred in the musical drama Dreamgirls *in 2006.*

Fun Facts

In the early days, Destiny's Child practiced at Beyoncé's mother's hair salon. Tina Knowles also designed the group's costumes.

Beyoncé and her Destiny's Child bandmates released solo music albums in 2002 and 2003. Beyoncé's first, *Dangerously In Love*, won five Grammy Awards in 2004. This tied the record for most Grammys won by a female artist at a single ceremony!

In 2010, Beyoncé went on to break the record for most Grammy wins (six) in one night for a female artist.

Beyoncé's reputation as a flawless performer makes almost everything she touches a success. Products she promotes sell out. Videos she makes for her music become **iconic**.

Beyoncé's fresh and clever approach to album releases and concerts sets her apart from many musical artists. She takes her time making albums and developing new concert "experiences."

With her second album, *B'Day*, she included a DVD of music videos. Her tour, called The Beyoncé Experience, featured an all-female band. Beyoncé often works together with other musicians. They include her husband, rap artist Jay-Z, and her sister Solange.

Beyoncé and Jay-Z

REINVENTING A SUPERSTAR

With her 2008 third album, *I Am... Sasha Fierce*, Beyoncé developed a musical **alter ego**. Sasha Fierce was more outspoken than Beyoncé. The character also helped her overcome stage fright.

Over time, Beyoncé decided she no longer needed an alter ego. Hard work gave her confidence.

With each new album, Beyoncé made new and **innovative** changes. Her 2013 album *Beyoncé* was a surprise **visual album**. Her album *Lemonade* was released in 2016 along with a film of the same name! In 2024, she issued a country music album called *Cowboy Carter*.

Cowboy Carter *explored the African American roots of country music.*

Beyoncé's concert tours are known for their electrifying atmosphere. She and her professional dancers train like Olympic athletes. The costumes, stage design, and theatrical presentation are all overseen by Queen Bey.

Fun Facts

Beyoncé has made 10 documentaries and films. She directed six of them. Some are about her concert tours. Others are about her life and interests, including **empowering** women and Black people.

LEGACY MAKER

Early in her career, Beyoncé focused on music. Awards and honors were great, but Beyoncé wanted more. As her fame grew, she used it to start other businesses, and to champion causes close to her heart.

Beyoncé has endorsed several perfumes. She has also released her own perfume brand.

One of Beyoncé's interests is fashion. In 2005, Beyoncé and her mother launched a fashion line called House of Deréon. Beyoncé has also teamed with many companies and fashion houses to produce or promote fashion lines.

Beyoncé is known as a style icon. She starts trends in music, fashion, and culture.

In 2010, Beyoncé founded Parkwood Entertainment. Named after the street she grew up on, Parkwood produces music, films, videos, and television specials. The company also manages other artists.

Beyoncé has launched many businesses on her own and with others. They include the music-streaming service Tidal and a sportswear line called Ivy Park.

Fun Facts

Beyoncé's first name is actually her mother's last name! Tina was born Celestine Beyoncé. Beyoncé has Louisiana **Creole** ancestry through her mother.

Beyoncé is known for her Midas Touch—everything she touches turns to gold. But she has always worked hard. Her **work ethic** helped make her one of the world's wealthiest music artists.

Sharing her wealth and influence is important to Beyoncé. She gives her time and money to causes she believes in. She founded the charity BeyGOOD. It grants money to small businesses and gives scholarships to students.

Beyoncé has supported many causes, including earthquake and flood relief, food banks, racial justice, and childhood diabetes research and care.

GLOSSARY

alter ego (AWL-ter EE-goh): An alternate self or different version of oneself

Creole (KREE-ohl): A person born in Louisiana who is a descendant of the original French settlers

destined (DES-tind): To be certain to do something or be something

endorse (en-DAWRS): To publicly say that you like a product in exchange for money

empowering (em-POU-er-ing): Giving power to someone

genres (ZHAHN-ruhs): Types or categories of music

Grammy Awards (GRAM-ee uh-WAWRDS): Awards given by the Recording Academy of the United States to recognize outstanding achievements in music

iconic (ahy-KON-ik): Something or someone celebrated and idolized as representing an era or culture

influential (in-floo-EN-shuhl): Having the power to influence the actions, behavior, or opinions of others

innovative (IN-uh-vey-tiv): Something that is new or original

reinventing (ree-in-VENT-ing): Making anew or making over in a different form

visual album (VIZH-oo-uhl AL-buhm): A record album that is released with a film or individual music videos for each song

work ethic (wurk ETH-ik): A belief that hard work is important and leads to success

INDEX

WEBSITES TO VISIT

https://www.beyonce.com

https://beygood.org

https://kids.britannica.com/students/article/Beyoncé/574400

ABOUT THE AUTHOR

Ellen Rodger won a bank-sponsored short story contest at age nine. It was the last thing her bank ever gave her for free, but it kicked-started a career in newspaper, magazine, and book publishing. Ellen has written hundreds of books for curious young people, on topics as varied as the history of the potato, urban wildlife, refugees, the Great Lakes, and explorers.

Crabtree Publishing

crabtreebooks.com 800-387-7650

Written by: Ellen Rodger
Designed by: Kathy Walsh
Series Development: James Earley
Editor: Melissa Boyce
Educational Consultant: Marie Lemke M.Ed.
Production manager: Candice Campbell

Hardcover: 978-1-0398-8041-2
Paperback: 978-1-0398-8401-4
Ebook (pdf): 978-1-0398-8161-7
Epub: 978-1-0398-8281-2

Printed in the U.S.A./CP2025

Published in Canada
Crabtree Publishing
616 Welland Ave.
St. Catharines, Ontario
L2M 5V6

Published in the United States
Crabtree Publishing
347 Fifth Ave
Suite 1402-145
New York, NY 10016

Library and Archives Canada Cataloguing in Publication
Available at Library and Archives Canada

Library of Congress Cataloging-in-Publication Data
Available at the Library of Congress

Photographs
Alamy: Rob Watkins p 9, mark reinstein p 11
Newscom: NC1/WENN, p 10, WENN English Top Features, 19, Guerin Charles/ABACA p 26,
Shutterstock: Tinseltown, cover, title page; Sky Cinema, TOC; Joe Seer, p 6;
Featureflash Photo Agency, p 7 (left), p 8 (middle), p 13, p 14, p 17, p 29; Everett Collection, p 7 (right), p 15, p 23, p 24, p 28; DFree, p 8 (top); udo salters photography, p 8 (bottom); Robert Hoetink, p 12 (top); Kraft74, p 12 (bottom); s_bukley, p 16 (middle), p 27; A.RICARDO, p 20, p 22 (bottom); Tinseltown, p 25
Wikimedia: Creative Commons, p 4, 5, 16 (top, bottom), 18, 22 (top)
All other images from Shutterstock